Cool Indy Cars

Jon M. Fishman

Lerner Publications ◆ Minneapolis

Lerner Publications Company
A division of Lerner Publishing Group, Inc.
241 First Avenue North
Minneapolis, MN 55401 USA

For reading levels and more information, look up this title at www.lernerbooks.com.

Library of Congress Cataloging-in-Publication Data

Names: Fishman, Jon M., author.
Title: Cool Indy cars / Jon M. Fishman.
Description: Minneapolis : Lerner Publications, 2019. | Series: Lightning bolt books. Awesome rides | Includes bibliographical references and index.
Identifiers: LCCN 2017041217 (print) | LCCN 2017046392 (ebook) | ISBN 9781541525061 (eb pdf) | ISBN 9781541519923 (lb : alk. paper) | ISBN 9781541527546 (pb : alk. paper)
Subjects: LCSH: Indy cars—Juvenile literature.
Classification: LCC TL236 (print) | LCC TL236 .F57 2019 (ebook) | DDC 629.228/5—dc23

LC record available at https://lccn.loc.gov/2017041217

Manufactured in the United States of America
1-44328-34574-11/1/2017

Table of Contents

It's an Indy Car!

Vroom! A pack of Indy cars zips around a curve in a racetrack. The drivers grip their steering wheels. They zoom toward the finish line.

Indy cars are race cars. Drivers race Indy cars on many different racetracks. Sometimes they even race on public streets.

Indy cars compete in IndyCar Series races. Drivers win points depending on what place they finish in these races. The driver with the most points each season is named the champion.

The IndyCar Series champion receives $1 million in prize money.

The Indianapolis 500 is the most famous race of the IndyCar Series. Indy cars are named after this race. Drivers zoom around a 2.5-mile (4 km) track two hundred times to finish the race.

The Indianapolis 500 takes place at the Indianapolis Motor Speedway in Indianapolis, Indiana.

The Indy Car Story

Indy car racing began in 1911. That was the first year of the Indianapolis 500. Forty cars raced for more than $14,000 in prize money.

Ray Harroun's car design became the regular design for Indy cars.

Racer Ray Harroun designed a special car for the first Indianapolis 500. Most race cars at the time carried two people. Harroun's car had room for just one person.

The Indianapolis 500 has been canceled only six times since 1911.

The first Indianapolis 500 was a big hit with fans. The race became a popular yearly event.

IndyCar formed in 1994. The organization oversees the IndyCar Series. IndyCar sets up events and creates rules for Indy car races.

Indy Car Parts

Rrr! Rrr! A crew member puts thick tires on an Indy car. The rear tires are bigger than the front tires.

A narrow body and small front tires help this car cut through the air and go faster.

Indy cars are built especially for racing. They have a narrow body and a thin nose.

Indy cars have wide, flat wings in the front and the back. Wind rushes over the wings and pushes the car to the ground.

Wings help an Indy car's tires grip the racetrack.

The driver's head sticks above the car as it zooms around the track. The engine is behind the driver. An Indy car's engine can make 500 to 700 horsepower.

Indy Cars in Action

There are plenty of thrills at an Indy car race. The cars streak by at amazing speeds. You may miss the action if you don't keep your eyes on the track!

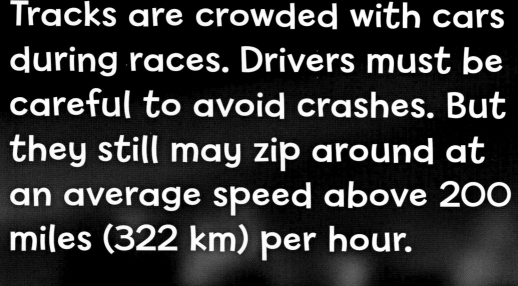

Tracks are crowded with cars
during races. Drivers must be
careful to avoid crashes. But
they still may zip around at
an average speed above 200
miles (322 km) per hour.

An Indy car can go more
than 230 miles (370 km)
per hour on an open track.

An Indy car drives into a pit stop. Crew members rush out to change the car's tires and fill it with gas. Then the car hurries back to the race.

A pit stop takes only about eight seconds!

Indy car racing is growing. IndyCar has plans to hold races in countries around the world. Soon fans will have even more chances to see the fastest cars in auto racing.

Indy Car Diagram

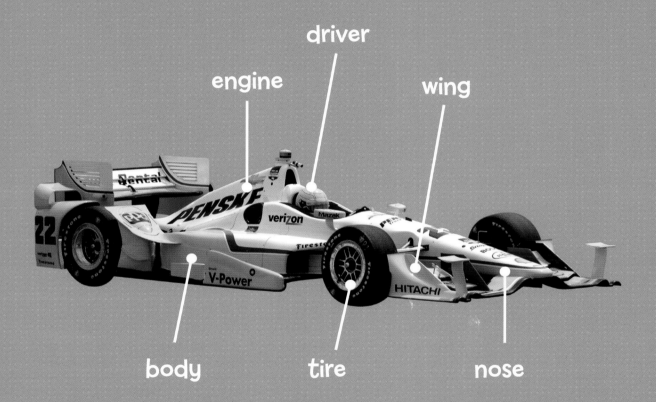

driver

engine

wing

body

tire

nose

Indy Car Facts

- The winner of the Indianapolis 500 drinks milk to celebrate the win. Race winner Louis Meyer started the tradition in 1936.

- Indy car races can be seen on TV in more than two hundred countries.

- Ray Harroun invented the rearview mirror to use in the Indianapolis 500. He needed it to see behind him since he was the only person in the car.

Glossary

body: the main outside part of a car

crew member: a person such as a mechanic who works on Indy cars

design: to make something according to a plan

horsepower: a unit that measures the power of an engine. The term *horsepower* comes from comparing the power of an engine to the power of one horse.

nose: the front tip of a race car

prize money: money given as an award for winning a race or a race series

wing: a long, narrow piece on the front or back of a car that uses air to push the car to the ground

Further Reading

Crane, Cody. *Race Cars*. New York: Children's Press, 2018.

Early Cars: Fact Sheet for Children
https://www.si.edu/Encyclopedia_SI/nmah
/earlycars.htm

Indianapolis 500
https://kids.kiddle.co/Indianapolis_500

Indianapolis Motor Speedway Kids Club
http://www.indy500kids.com

Lanier, Wendy Hinote. *Indy Cars*. Lake Elmo, MN: Focus Readers, 2017.

Silverman, Buffy. *How Do Formula One Race Cars Work?* Minneapolis: Lerner Publications, 2016.

Index

Photo Acknowledgments

The images in this book are used with the permission of: HodagMedia/Shutterstock.com, pp. 2, 4, 5, 6, 11, 12, 15, 18, 19, 23; Carol M. Highsmith Archive/Library of Congress (LC-DIG-highsm-40835), p. 7; Library of Congress (LC-DIG-ggbain-11279), p. 8; Bettmann/Getty Images, p. 9; Bibliothèque nationale de France/Wikimedia Commons (Public Domain), p. 10; Ty Hill/Wikimedia Commons (CC BY-SA 3.0), p. 13; Michael Allio/Icon Sportswire/Newscom, p. 14; Rainier Ehrhardt/Getty Images, p. 16; Jared C. Tilton/Getty Images, p. 17; © Walter/flickr.com (CC BY 2.0), p. 20.

Cover: Jeffrey Brown/Icon Sportswire/Getty Images.

Main body text set in Billy Infant regular 28/36. Typeface provided by SparkType.